Re-emergence

Sofia Khan

Copyright © 2010 by Sofia Khan

All rights reserved. No part of this book may be reproduced or utilized in any form or by any means, electronic or mechanical, including photocopying, recording or by any information storage and retrieval system, without permission in writing from the publisher.

Printed in the United States of America

First Edition, 2011

Library of Congress Control Number: 2011901165

ISBN 978-0-9832442-2-6

Cover design by tatlin.net

www.sofiakhan.com

To my mother and father –
You made me know what it's like
To be a princess.

Together, we soar high and realize
The truest blessings.

Contents

From the Author   ix

Preface   xiii

Conversation with Time   3

A Point of Light   33

Snowy Day in Houston   65

A Test of Faith   75

Moments Worth Waiting For   85

Dearest Path   91

Re-emergence   103

Credits and Acknowledgments   113

About the Author   115

From the Author

I wish to contribute to the search for a new way forward in times of need, to offer strength and to express feelings of hope through poetic conversation. The writing and the conversation throughout the book are combined to reach the reader in my own personal way of discovering so much.

I start in a state of inner turmoil, as written in the first chapter. I search for answers everywhere, and begin to find a new direction that leads to a better future.

Through this emotional journey, I progress and create a new world for myself. Each chapter reveals emotion as I approach my own re-emergence. I still have so much to experience, in this lifetime. It goes on.

Our lives, at times, are difficult. Within us, internal challenges might seem impossible to overcome. Something has changed for the worse, giving a sense that this circumstance has permanently attached itself to our existence. We are overwhelmed and yearn that the beauty of life will appear. The life of each individual, organization and nation has its own unique unforeseeable events, obstacles, misfortunes, and upsets. I see a part of my experience as a universal message about our human spirit and about the way forward.

Deep within us, we must rationalize that we are not trapped forever, and that any inner conflict we struggle with can be overcome. When we decide to conquer the conflicts, we approach the realization that it is our own choice that will determine the direction and decision for the future. As we move forward we live in a new way, through each experience – we encounter so many existing friends who are selfless, open, and willing to give freely. They are all there, waiting to share with us. Our true self emerges. We find that it was our own voice that we heard, that provided the guidance and direction.

My hope is to connect with each reader through the art of self-expression.

Preface

This moment alone, a memory surfaces…now…after so many years…my school teacher…
The only one in my school years
Who walked with me, she took me with her.
So in tune with me, holding my hand, she took me places
She loved me; I was her pride and joy, she wrote
In my report card
She understood me.
I couldn't see through her eyes, her character truthful

"Teach them, what I see in you," her heart was telling me

No spoken words

She gave her whole classroom to me, I knew not why

She gave me the material, books, whatever she had.

So generous, so understanding,

I knew not the words of her heart,

Spoken through graceful gestures

I asked myself, how…what…I'm me…

She trusted me completely, that I could teach my classmates.

This recollection crystallizes in my mind…today, in a new way.

It is all stored, the connection she shared with me.

Silently…as I search this universe within me.

"Show them what you're made of. I want them to see this world, the way you see it. Your unique qualities, the depth, the perception, that are so naturally yours."

I knew not how to verbalize myself then,

I was in second grade.

She gave me recognition

She rewarded me for using my gifts

She gave me a specific, well-defined task

To share of myself in my own way

There was no deadline, no limits. No urgency at that moment.

Is what she saw in me, the HOW of my existence?

Today…maybe this is how…

She was telling me…then…in her own way, without explanation

I wish I could have asked her:

"There is purpose in your intentions

The substance you see

It lies within me; invisible to the naked eye

I possess it so naturally; it's me.

Acknowledge its relevance to me

Reach this pure heart so I understand you –

Find the way to me – tell me in truths –

So I can give you exactly what you are telling me to do

Create the picture for me, paint with your words, of where you want me to go, with your feelings, with your Heart, and all that you possess, your thoughts, all your understanding, use your essence,

Connect with me, show me in the way you see me, on that wavelength –

You know me, you recognize me – the real me – it is your gift

Share it with me

What lies beneath my own surface will come to life with your message

I shall move forward in excellence."

Re-emergence

Conversation with Time

If you surrender only to truth,
You protect each tomorrow

"Oh time," I confided, "many years have passed. And I believe that I have lost my bearing. I am stuck in confusion, restlessness, and anguish. I didn't foresee this consequence - these forces that reside within me have overpowered and blockaded my vision. My heart speaks impatiently. Oh time, I must talk with you."

Time asked me,
"What needs to be solved to make your world better?"

Without pause, time continued, "What was it that you listened to?

And, what was it that you chose?"

"Did you ever ask yourself the simple question –
- What will happen tomorrow,
    And the next day,
    And the day after that, once I choose?"

And then, time posed another piece of the puzzle, "Have you considered listening, really closely, to the words of that wise man?"

"<u>When</u> will you listen?" asks time. "<u>When</u> will it be too late?"

"Have you ever really taken <u>me</u>, to listen?" *said in a whisper.*

Silence. My head lowers, nodding solemnly, as if...."I have not taken <u>you</u>, at all. Only, for granted."

Oh time, these riddles posed to me – swimming in my head – how could I possibly not know you? Yet I've lived all these years, without knowing you at all, never before examining you…this is my first time conversing in this way.

Time responds – "Let's take some of _me_, let's see if I can reach you so you can gradually realize who I am. Your mind races in every direction, and has caused a chaotic blur. Before I start to explain myself, be reassured that you have me. I am yours. Every breath, every blink, every movement, your thoughts, your feelings, every second…I'm there. I am TIME."

I ask, "Time, where are you taking me?"

Without hesitation, time corrects me, "No…it is <u>YOU</u> that takes me. I'm a gift, given to you.

This…me…know me."

Time goes on, "I'm with you. You choose. The how, where, what, when, why, who…I'm with you all the way."

Time explains, "Now that we're having this dialog, I will introduce myself to you, a little more. It may take you a long while to understand me, sometimes up to the last breath.

I am infinite

You are sensing me today as finite, and for once you want my response, a dire urgency at hand

I go

One direction

One destination

Forward

Non-stop

I wait not.

I belong to all. Everywhere.

I'm with you, every moment, and beyond

I flash before your eyes, maybe once or twice

I'm silent – you call on me at the most critical moment

You are free to use me as you choose – a blessing

I reveal truths, answers, beauty

I am the same – I withstand all tests

Always

Every moment

In silence – I'm still there

I am the only forever – I am purity in its most misunderstood abundance in creation.

No one escapes me, nothing is without me.
Every star, every galaxy, each brushstroke of life's masterpiece
All through me
I am beyond measuring

Every heart that beats
It is heard by me…I listen quietly
Every cry, every cheer, laughter
Emotion, every murmur, all that's living.

Those moments – the memorable ones –
The heart skips in passion
The heart races
It pounds
When in tune with <u>me</u>, the heart loses all track of <u>me</u>
 Through victory
              success
              realization
              faith
              love
              accomplishment
              creativity
              beauty
              energy
The heart aligns with me, as one.

This dimension,
I am of the essence
I am the most precious of all gifts bestowed upon you,
The most silent
The best friend, that does not disagree with you
More precious than all the gold on earth –

> Ah…gold, that gold
> That vein of gold
> Rare, noble element, mystical, perpetual
> Well traveled beyond this galaxy
> Supernatural forces
> Untarnished
> Hidden within the layers
> …All through me."

Time asks, "this gift, am I valued?
Perhaps ignored altogether…time…"
I reflect on the voice that comes from my heart.
To time, I respond – "Over and over again,
I find myself saying to the universe, when I'm alone,
'Find me.'
I call out, 'Where am I?
What am I doing here?'
These crowds…this unlit, dreary, weary, dull, dim,
desolate space I'm locked in

Oh time, I have to do something

I'm anxious, unsure, pacing, waiting…

I have faith

There must be a way to get there, I have to get there.

Time, you keep going on, I stay lost

I'm reminded, over and over,

I'm haunted by my own existence.

Oh life,

Oh time,

My regret…slow motion, slowly,

Slipping…to where…

I know not…

Where, when…

Existence itself…that moment, inevitable

It has all reached my heart."

Time interrupts with knowing words, "Yes, your heart

pulls

tears

weeps

whispers to me -

> Time, please stop, turn back, or I'll break.
>
> Whatever you say, oh time,
>
> I will do it
>
> Just tell me,
>
> I will do it."

I continue, "Oh time,

that moment came…

there was a moment…

oh life…you've thrown such an odd curveball.

This was the moment when I realized

YOU

And all I could say, in all of my anguish,

At the thought…

All I could say was…

'I never listened to him,'" sobbing.

Time responds softly, "You misunderstood,

You were limited, it's not easy reaching that destination

You knew not of this journey of heart and me,

I'm still with you –

I'm here, I'm not gone,

Use me – I'm still here,

I will be with you through it all,

Whether you know it or not –

There is no replacement for me –

No alternative

Through me, anything is possible…you choose

Use me…I'm yours

Take me…I am time."

Time continues – "I've explained to you,
It's your choice, so the HOW is up to you.
This gift of time, your heart is telling you
DO SOMETHING...*listen to love, listen to life, wisdom*
Why wait? Why?
Your heart has said ENOUGH. It spoke.
When your heart speaks, I will never oppose it
When you choose, there is no lingering
It's done, in that moment of me.
You've asked WHEN?
                    HOW MUCH LONGER?
These are mere moments that come, then go.
Use all of me. Your most precious gift.
You're so concerned, you're not moving –
Stricken with wasted emotion.
In response to your questions –
There is a natural course through me; events unfold.
Your heart, full of grief, anguish, pain...
Yes...your heart will feel this
The life all around you will provide softness,
If you choose to live it.

        The rays of the sun beaming, then vanish
        Sheer clouds whispering to the moon, veiled
        Stars glittering, one by one
        Each season has its own rare delights
        Living among the living, with me...oh heart.

Time continues, "Take me
            use me
                      give me away as a gift to loved ones
      Connect this heart of yours, as you choose
      Reconcile all pains in peace and action
      Give of self, without self in mind, solve your world's problems

Surrender, listen to your heart, in _me_
      NO MORE – this is the truth. NOW.
      Spend me – on you, if you choose to.
      I am of the essence
      If you choose to use _me_ to know what all you possess,
      Perhaps the answers will appear, in _me_.
      Whatever appears as truth,
      Examine them over me,
      Use me, align your heart with me.

Beat as one with me.
      Seek in every possible way, go higher, and further
      Go to your destination. Be precise about where you want to go. It's all that counts – the result.
      It will require _me_ – to get there.
      There is no stopping.

This reality is the challenge.
> When you walk on the path with wisdom,
> Indeed, the ultimate treasure of life
> Seeking, hunting, takes <u>me</u>, all your life.
> With <u>me</u>, and with wisdom, you will align onto
> your own path."

"This treasure chest – it never empties –
> always abundant
> full of truth

>> It will tell you straight –
>> guide you
>> show you

The truth will appear in front of you
It will face you and openly present
The answers to all of what you seek,
The way to go; your heart will speak and listen.

You will know.

It's <u>time</u> to live – your way. NOW.
There is no other way – it's your own.
I'm yours.

You and me – we could be something so beautiful –
  Use me to go where you belong
  Feel yourself emerge,
  It's never too late
  Go on, go forward, in a new way, your own.

It won't take forever
But if you don't choose it
You will never know – a lost dream.
All it takes is
You
You may feel that you're losing me – a waste
NO.
This is the price you pay. A requirement
It is the only way. Start paying
NOW
Use me*!*
Go back to that fork in the road
as I move forward – we both go, as one, as you find the way.
Start living, once more, as one, with me.
As you. Be you.

That treasure chest in open sight
A heartbeat away
Within your reach, all your life
So abundant, so rich, so rare
Yet you've run from it,
This complexity you've created, you've chosen,
It has solutions. A daunting challenge.
I ask you again,

"Have you ever really taken <u>me</u>, to LISTEN?"
Time whispers

After pondering, I respond,
    "I have thought of myself as a good listener
    For the first time I will have to decide on a new
    way to listen, carefully. Through you.
    I can do it, I do listen, and I also believe in
    action."

Time explains,
    "Only TRUTH stands upright.
    This truth – you will find it when your heart
    Beats as one with mine, on and on.
    It will not let you down, ever.
    It will lift you up; you will solve the complexity.

Only you can choose the right way.

It's the truth.

There are no corners you can cut
Go back – it's the only way
You owe it to yourself

Spend <u>me</u>; the more you spend, the richer you become

Forgive yourself for the mistakes you have made

For getting on this road that you have chosen
A road that was destined for your current state of mind,
From the moment you chose it

Did you have this creation in mind,
Then?

If you feel crowded, walk faster
> Go to your destination that waits
>> NOW
>> Pass the crowd
>> Into the clearance
>> Forge your way, in the spirit of the pioneer
>> Whose pride is its constructive forces
>> That cannot be bought with gold or silver
>> The pioneer pays the intangible price
>> All through me, in truth

No sorrows, enough apologies, come home.

I say: "To understand truth...I want to be sure..."
Time replies – "Maintain your true identity – there is only one.

And that is the whole truth.
> Reveal it
> Search for it
> Say to yourself –
> FIND ME*!*
> It is you – crying out*!*

The right path is your own, where you will find yourself
Where the true self lives –
Peace, serenity
Love, flowing abundantly
From where you prepare to face the world each day
That gives you the strength to go out and get it done
The truth
The wisdom
All can line your path, wherever you go, on your way.
Birthplace of new thoughts, ideas of all kinds
At home
The heart

A new world emerges, before you know it."

I engage, "Oh time,
I don't want the night to end
This dialog with you, there is so much you give to me
My mind is expanding with new thinking
The depth of your words, penetrating yet defying my senses

You are reaching me…I am grasping the message you bring

I admit, I have much to overcome, in my current state of mind

Your patience is appreciated

You know me, you know what is at stake

I could go on and on with you…"

Time replies – "There is much more to do,

                      to learn

                      to seek

Use me, build upon these words

This new world that emerges

Does not overwhelm the senses

It is acquired naturally, gracefully as one with me

A life of its own

Live in all ways that you can

Your mind will never get full

There is room for more

All the way to the sky, the heavens, go further

Keep going. Don't stop.

Go forward, as I do

As one"

Time speaks, "Truth – live by it
The power of truth
I'll give you an example, when it comes to me…
NEVER
FOREVER
Study closely and know what they mean –
Such extremes – so powerful

Truth…
Revealed in time
Knocking down previous beliefs
New thoughts, new ideas, progressing forward
All created here, in this world
All through me

Go forward. In the right direction.
New thoughts arise
New solutions
Possibilities exist through me
Your world is in crisis, you are calling to me
Your pain froze you,
Storms, turmoil – all because of what?
Is it the road that you are on?
Does each aspect line up?
Every angle, every facet, each clue, each theory,
Each claim, each assertion? All?

Everything in your power will solve it
You may think of one approach – maybe two –
Only the truth will stand. All else disappears.
Only the results count.

The truth will unlock all chains
                      all barriers
                      all doors
It's a matter of choice…
With all the wisdom, the truth staring you in the face,
What will you do?"

I admit, "Oh time, I must seek the truth of this matter.
There is so much depth in what you say, my mind is
challenged by your message. I choose to listen…please,
go on."

"Take off. Go where you are able to solve it.
It's time to solve this matter
Use me and go back to that junction
Trace your steps through me
You will reach your destination
The signs, the clues, will all point you to the answer…

You decide –

Your world –

Full of voices

Billions of voices –

How can you possibly decide among these voices?

Leave the crowds

Walk faster – away. Forward.

Only then,

Will you begin to hear the sound of your heartbeat,

Will you be able to grasp wisdom and truth.

Choices abundant –

One truth.

In <u>me</u> – all truths revealed.

Something is needed NOW.

When you tell yourself to DO IT,

You have my full cooperation, my permission

Granted.

To choose the truth –

You will have to overcome the obstacles

of NEVER

    FOREVER

Only I am of these extremes - I am time*!*

In me, as you choose in truth,
There is no lingering, no wavering,
As though the stars line up all for you
As you move forward
To reach your destination

Think beyond
The future awaits your arrival
What you choose today, now
Determines a new beginning
Every moment

If you surrender only to truth,
You protect each tomorrow
For your own existence
For your world
For now
And forward
Strength, courage
Challenge each opposition with a new way
Specific goals
All you possess – open the mind
Use it to create this vision

The choice, with wisdom and truth
You lead. Take me there – to your vision"

Time says –

"This life you were created for, to live

Spend me all up

Find yourself

No more cries

What will I reveal to you after you spend me?

Every layer, hidden beneath the surface

Uncovered

Wiped away

You will be face to face with truth, the way to go

And your heartbeat as one with me

Envision the foundation of your existence

Without thoughts of the past

The past…

It is simply GONE

Wasting me on the past does not bring your wealth.

Action

You have to go forward to build your internal wealth

It is the only way, with <u>me</u>, to be your best

I cannot go in any other direction

Use <u>me</u> to create

        innovate

        renew

        strengthen

        survive

        thrive

Once you reach the destination,

Your reward is great

Your heart will beat as one with your most precious gift

– <u>me</u>.

The knowing, the feeling, the sensation –

The joy in your heart will bring tears

In private moments

As you face the heavens

You'll say, 'It's me.'

You will tell me –

'Oh time, I gave you all I had,

All

Every breath

Every drop

My strength

My will

The determination

My focus

My perception

My understanding

My body

My sweat

These hands

This power

I did what I set out to do
In excellence
In truth
With integrity
I gave and gave and gave some more
I pushed,
I went on,
I burned
Past each day, each night
I listened
I learned
I created
I used all senses,
All gifts
All talents
I did not quit
I had to get there
I will never give less
This is my way
And that is what I'm made of.'

Time says – "No other pride matters.
Lay your tracks all over me!
Excel. Achieve. Advance.

It is up to you – the rewards are there, waiting for you, in every direction, on the right path
It's your destination –
Will you unlock these talents, dormant,

                        stored,

                        waiting?

Why wait…do you even know or remember what you possess?

The gifts are there

Search, survey

Unravel them

Detect what remains within

Go through each layer

Each layer a different unique signature

Examine, interpret

Use the right tools, the right methods

Set the right goals to maintain freedom, independence

Of your true identity

So that it will flow naturally as you go on

Declare the way

Claim it

And solve this complexity in your world

Use me, no waste

Directly detect it. Illuminate that richness within you, head on

Extract it

This treasure awaits its discovery –

It's right here

Not on faraway shores

Empower the entire being and solve it

With all talents, all resources, all you possess

Lead the way, clear the path, overcome all obstacles

Trust it

Inspire it

Aim high

A lasting reward will follow

This is your destination.

This is living. Through me.

And you will say,

"It's me…"

Perhaps you cannot see.

The mind of the genius sees all

Every angle, every tomorrow

Genius does exist, like a rare, beautiful, exotic gem.

Beneath your surface – all is found.

It's the HOW

Which will be the challenge

This HOW – a new way forward, from today and on

Will you <u>LISTEN</u> to the one who says…

'I have the answer'

Each and every time, in truth, standing alone,
So honest and upright…who will listen?" asks time.

"And who will be brave enough to accept the truth?"

Time says to me, finally:

>"Your heart rules you –
>It is your heart that needs to flow
>Harmoniously
>Abundantly,
>Full

Your life – that one that is your own
>Its own imprint
>Original
>One of a kind throughout the history of time
>In this universe

It will be created around your own heartbeat
As you travel on your own path,
That will be as one with me,
When you are on the right road, in this lifetime.
It's time to go home."

Whispering, time says…go back,
>*you're on the wrong road*
>*What your heart desires, is not here*
>*Use me…if you choose to*
>*I'm precious to you – I'm time.*

A Point of Light

Do not waste your precious time worshipping me!
I am not the destination!

A dark, heavy journey, weary winding pathways, leading to what sort of destination – suddenly from where appears a heavenly magic star? This point of light – out of my reach and so overpowering to my senses – I know not how to thank, to welcome, to just glimpse at – never before imagining of its very existence.

Always reaching out to me.

It grabbed me inside

It lingers on and on – why?

Unexpectedly. I found you – your glow,
    the warmth,
    the radiance

To reveal all I have thought about you –
    would take more than this lifetime

This long journey – in the darkness – seeing you,
    I'm home – I cannot do anything but drop these
    heavy bags and run to you
    Do you even know what you've done?

I thought – will I ever find my way home?
Can I achieve this?

Oh light, stay, don't go…I know not when we shall meet again – when I see you – I think…this may be the last time

The light: brilliant yet soft
    direct without cutting like a laser
    lively and inviting
    captivating, yet focused on its work at hand
    Illumination

When I saw the light, I said…this is it.

Looking straight at you, under your spell…
I'm leaving this dreary desolation.
I have to change my life…I was motionless. Still.
It was sudden, I did not plan this thought,
I was alive, I was awake, I could see all around me,
The light gave me the power to see clearly

Oh light, you know not what you did –
I never revealed it directly to you, I did not have a talk with you to tell you that I was going through so many changes,
Living in darkness.
There is so much to see.

A burning flame melts the wax
The wax flows, in its liquid form, over time forms new shapes, new creations
This flame re-creates character into what was once a plain, thin, taper.
New life form, unique
Realization

What did I cut myself off from, all these years?
…myself.
peace
excellence

I want to reach my destination – it is somewhere else –
I will find myself, only then, only there, whole.

I want only a few things – they are not possessions, nor can they be possessed – they are elements

the warm breeze of a summer evening, to watch the sun set and witness the first star appearing at the twilight, I want to see fire in the eyes, a desire in the heart and soul, a voice that sounds like no other, a look that strengthens, the feel of the dust and dirt all over my body after a long, hot bike ride, the toil and sweat that comes from exerting mind and body, a little admiration, a little affection, the feel of sand between my toes as I look for shells on the seashore, the sound of the waves, birds singing, pigeons and doves flapping wings, the green and glistening as I ride through the trees, the rhythm of the music, the mystique of a wooden flute that has brought out energizing creativity and taken me to centuries past.

- my mind heals and clears through all of this time spent moving in a new direction

- I may be alone, but I don't feel any sense of hollowness – I made the decision once the light showed itself

Emotions consume me – Prayers of hope
                of wishes
                no pity
                of thanking

Desire to improve, to simplify, to grow in positive ways, shed anything that weighs me down –
The weight –
    guilt
    junk
    aggravation
    anger
    waste

Replace with life that is clear
                      smooth
                      warm
                      flowing
                      bubbly
                      light
                      free
                      straight
                      open
                      deep

It happened unexpectedly. Then I decided.

Light told me – true love exists.

> Time waits for no one.
> To be something good, you'll have to pay the price.
> Justice will be rendered.
> Believe in destiny.
> Get on the right path – turn around – there is nothing to fear
> Understand truth
> Seek wisdom
> Listen to the wise man.

What was it? Was I being guided by a force outside of my realm – or only circumstance?

> prayer?
> fulfillment?
> desire?
> dissatisfaction?

Was I at the crossroads of my life?

"It is now that you will see – what all you can be. In your own way. Not like me. <u>Like you</u>. There's no one else like you. There is only one of you, just like I'm also one, unique in this universe. This is not a contest of you and me. Be who you are. I'm a friend. With a message."

Light – gives perception

Light, what do you possess that was able to affect me so greatly, how did you reach me?
>	You are reassuring
>	I'm drawn to you
>	I'm in awe
>	I'm inspired
>	We are face to face

Are you working on me, are you demanding from me, what are these skills you possess, what gift allows you to connect, where does this brilliance and focus come from, this endurance you have, your commitment, this devotion of your very being?

What can I do for you in return? What sort of impact do I make, I'm not so good. Give me a chance – no, I'm not even prepared, don't give me your attention, I don't deserve it…I have nothing to show, compared to you.

>	I'm in this dark cell,
>	Now you've shone my way,
>	I need some time to grasp my bearings
>	To see with new eyes,
>	To learn, to seek, to understand,

> To look deeply
> I see the door – I will walk through it
> and I will go forward.

This hollow chamber – now filling with the light from your fire, I see movement, I see life. From within you. I feel my true self is coming.

You are there; sometimes I cannot dare look at you, even though I feel the presence. Why do I feel I don't deserve to utter a noise? I remain silent, still, calm, -- your expression – it fills me – when you go, I miss you.

This journey of mine – this darkness –
The light won me over – showed me
I encountered it after not knowing
Somehow it pierced my heart.

Can there really be light?
What makes it so?
What is it – starlight
> sunlight
> moonlight?
> Some other force?
> Some other energy?
> Some other dimension that truly exists?

Living in self-made darkness, choices, consequences,
On some sort of pendulum –
> I've swung from hell to heaven.
> This new realm – is it an inch I've travelled?
>> in the right direction?
> Could there be miles?
> Could walking out of hell be heavenly in itself?
> Having light – is that the heaven? Just to see?
> Was it sent from heaven?
> Is the light the message?
> Is it the answer?
> The guide?
> A shining example of possibilities?

What do I do with this light?
> Will it fade?
> How can I hold onto it? I cannot.
> Was it a gift to me?
> "The time has come"
> How did it grip me in this way?

Light, are you here to <u>heal me</u>?
>> my blindness
>> shortsightedness
>> shed light on my life?

Light has renewed me.

I'm fascinated
Unspoken mystery in air when I can see.
So little time – the impact so great.

One instant; I knew.

You reached me in a split second
Were you watching me, waiting for the moment?
Was it by chance? Perhaps you have no knowledge of it at all

What was my reaction – did you invade my most private space? My doubts, my grievances, heart-stricken fears, You are so pure, so concentrated, you can sense everything with truth.

Something so true as light – I connected to truth through you, it was so honest. Honesty, clarity, felt so good.

There's so much more in this light, in truth, honesty, revealing everything.

Even if no one else can see – <u>you</u> somehow know,
Oh light, it is all clear to you –

You ask me – "why are you suffering today
>   why so much grief
>   why do you put on this brave front?
>   All I have to do is watch. Soon when no
>   one is around,
>   you will shed your tears,
>   you try holding everything inside –
>   No – I know all realities –

There is a way.

I will continue to shine

I will care when you ask not.

You will hear the sound of my voice
And you will find the strength to
Create your life to be more like me –"

A shining example

Complexities have solutions

Light says: "I give all I have within me
To come up with the right answer.

Until your last breath –
Use this point of light,

Seek your own honest answers –"
        These gifts – how can I use what I have?
                possess from within?
        Why have I wasted time without fully navigating
all there is to be accomplished?
        Why are they buried somewhere within –
            This treasure I possess?
        Am I ensnared by my own doing?
In how many ways do I know to express myself?
And do I?
Am I living or am I withering away?
What matters most?
Who have I not listened to their wisdom?
When will I set my own course and do all the right things
For myself?

Isn't it <u>ME</u> that has the ability to think
        beautiful thoughts where everything and
        everyone is lovely, deserving of praise,
        wanting kindness. I'm unique –

Turning even beggars into kings – in my eyes.
See beyond what appears to be.
Beyond obvious.

Part of the journey – if it is already written –
>   then it includes this passage from dark
>   to light, from feeling trapped to wanting
>   to be free, from taking life for granted
>   to understanding the time dimension, from
>   mundane to extraordinary

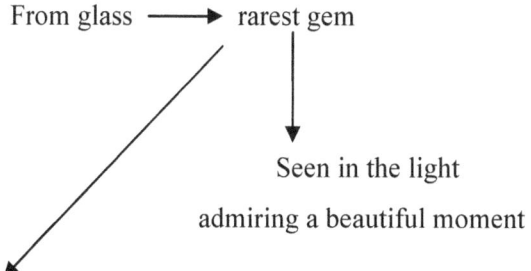

From glass ⟶ rarest gem

Seen in the light
admiring a beautiful moment

Such a gift to the soul

Light, if I don't see you again, how can I express
this sort of loss?

Even imagining it – tears at my strength to go on.
The separation, then to reunite after so long

Hardest to face – I turn away – so emotions remain
unseen.

In your presence, though, I forget for that moment, even if it is reality, and am entranced all over again – just to be within distance of you
Your light has softness, warmth of a gentle spirit that makes me feel I've been alive at some other time, and we are now revisiting that previous life, a re-discovery but with new identities.

> I recognize you, as though I knew you once, before, it is my secret. This time travel baffles even me.
>
> Is my mind – my own – tricking me?

Through you I see higher hopes for myself –
I see the goodness of life, there is a serenity, a feeling of being at home.

> You appear as happy as I am, when our paths cross
>
> So energized, you light up the room. I wish I was the reason for such expression. So dramatic!

Oh light – what takes your breath away?

Do I find some sort of comfort here? Seeing you?
You make it all better.
I look all around and know you are with me.

Do you hear me?

Your fire is burning in me – you lit my flame –

Now I'm warm inside

Everything has changed.

Light, I want to see.
Do you know what impact you have?
Why am I so slow to see?
Since I've seen the light, I'm floating
What is this effect?
    Better life
    Better future
  What's taking me there? Away from the past?

Oh life – I am getting my chance – Another.
Over and over, the light appears – directly,
not always with a smile, serious, straightforward.

All I really want is to make contact.

    No words. I wouldn't know what to say.

Just…I exist. You exist.

    There is something between us.

It will never be more, nor less.

    "You will go on, changed."

This light has the power to change it all.

One wish I had – it was about seeing this light in natural daylight – to look into the eyes of truth – with the flickering speckles from sunlight – could I be hypnotized even more than I already am, to follow this point of light?

Who sent you?

Did I need alignment onto another path?

You've existed – always have – this is my first experience – I haven't seen anything like you – right in full view, in front of me. Just when I needed you the most – here you are.

I admit – I was seeking some form of intelligence I knew
I was missing – until I saw for myself, I didn't know
how much I could feel.
It's too much, overwhelming – it's all new, I'm waking
up – thoughts – possibilities – imagination – inside me –
dancing – rising – refreshed after an arduous draining
labor
Everything new, colors bursting, energized
I go on.
It was heavy. I felt closed in. Caged.
   No trust
   Gloom
   Shadows

There is a time that will come, and it will be my time.
       Work has to be done. All kinds of work.
       But this work – I will bask in it,
       I will enjoy
       It will flow effortlessly
       It will seem so natural
       I will use the gifts – each of us has a reservoir
       full of them – our own riches

Finding strength

Contact brief, swift, time stands still at those moments as I'm drawn in by the attention
I get very still, taking in every detail, every movement, each moment.

I must learn
        study
        apply my mind
        creative spirit
        my will
You – strong will
        driven
        powerful force

This is what I see – I trust what I can see so clearly – this is the power you have
Some things – I may never say openly – even to you – the genius in you knows what has had the most impact on me.

The floating – the elevation – the dreaming –
what is it that causes such a phenomenon?
Lack of control?
A chance to travel? To fly? To examine?
Weakness? Strength? Misunderstanding?
Disguised emotion? Unspoken, silent, deep?
Influence?

Vulnerability?	Creative force
Addictive behavior?	Inspiration
Naivety?	
Foolishness?	

Or is this the way to receive, in this state of mind?

Tap into inner forces and discover what possibilities exist?

Which one is the reality?

This light – loved and admired, captivating, leading to obsession. The aura brings even thunder.

I see my own deficiencies when I can see this point of light, allowing me to be led to a safer path. It was a jolt, leaving me dazed yet very aware of my own errors – next to your perfection.

This unspoken jolt – it's all out of my hands, I cannot fight something so big. You're the one who could see this anguish – the depth of it – it has not been spoken of nor have I shared it openly – it manifests itself through other ways. Words don't express all feelings, all thoughts, the depth, the pain, the joy – the eyes say more – tears flow

      smiles
      love
      pain
      endurance
      concern   the
      honesty   knowing
      Eyes reveal so much -   genius

There will never be a goodbye, I cannot say it to you. But if I see you again each time I will have to silently thank you for being who you are, the shining example in my life – you handed me the key that unlocked my cell, and I walked out.

A Point of Light

My own day of tornado activity – you watched me, observing like a case study – the mood came to the surface. That day, your charm, your happiness – the forces within me – I probably wiped out your brightness completely.

Creating shadows that lingered on.
To this day I have not explained it.
My thoughts proved to be. I felt certain flaws.
I was correct.

We have gone on, those decisions are now filed away in a box somewhere.

Even keeping my composure – all is revealed before you. Your sensitivity – you study all.

I'm only human – I'm feeling so many of your effects;
I'm touched by you.
How did it come to be – searching
                    just opening eyes
                    you reached me
         That moment came --- CLICK
                    in a split second.

What is it, and what do you want from me?

All you've done is shine in my direction
and a transformation has occurred.

Parallel forces – love, desire
        time – stands still, ends, life
        <change>
        internal energy, wisdom, realization
            choice
            { acceptance
              truths }

- Purification
- transformation
-

All I ever wanted, since seeing for the first time, was for our eyes to continue to meet. That is my only wish. In itself, a great and beautiful gift. You read me; I strengthen, discover, I journey into the heart and soul. Me…drifting, full of love, unsettled, heart that the beat goes unheard, except by time, over time…my touch is unfelt

How did this light lift this spirit, how did you reach for me? Energize me? Give me a smile? I know nothing –

I know nothing of reason, of the few moments I've had in this condition.

I can only write now, that I'm on my way to a better day and better life. I feel better about myself, just knowing that this point of light is there, existing – a possibility for happiness.
Positive emotion

Am I stuck on you?
Are you some thing like a signal or code?
For a better life and world?
All that is true and strong and right?
I don't have answers.
You've been   my light
                    my inspiration
                    my positive force
                    energy
                    connection to a decision
          You possess an ingredient – intoxicating.
                  kindred spirit
                  another passerby

You've put me in touch with myself, my own qualities
<small>Father</small> – Keep going, don't stop
Some unusual bond – point of light
      closeness
Complete yourself!
Use all of it – what you possess.
It will drive by itself if you just use it.

Do not resist by holding on to the past.
Freedom, space, potential
Time – precious – now leave here and go find it all

This point of light – took me a long while to figure out what I saw – the message is clear now, only now – not then, when I experienced the actual encounter.

"Go beyond.

Think deeply, seek truth.

In truth, develop wisdom

Through wisdom, flourish and succeed

Be decisive, strong

Face tough challenges, move forward

Fulfill your purpose

Find the way to achieve your dreams

You have the patience, you have the faith.

Learn what you will need

Focus on the good.

Find the wavelength that offers a gentle grace, a calm yet vibrant energy, a fluidity – in order to gain and grasp knowledge

You will excel with will-power – and you will clear away (maneuver through) the hurdles thrown at you and replace them with thoughts and feelings that will lift up to the sky as you move forward.

Test your strength."

Light told me – finally:

"Do not waste your precious time worshipping me!
Do not cling to me!
My purpose has been to give you a way to seek realities and directions

I reach you so you can use me – see, seek, find
I am the purest form of illumination
Line your eyesight on your future, use me to go there.

There is no reason to stay as you are,
You found me, see where you are,
It is time to travel, to go on, to your destination.

Use all your talents, discover them in time
What stops you?

> These gifts – don't ever refuse to accept a gift that is given with so much thought – it has been bestowed upon you with love, generosity, in the spirit of sharing, each gift unique and suitable.

Your own talents
I am not the destination!

I am a means of getting there.
I'm your friend. I see pain, resistance, fear, uncertainty
This light, I know…you won't open up to me
This is new for you
You are overwhelmed, feeling lost until I appear,
Now you are speechless, in awe, you are humbled by my brilliance

Now you are able to see where you are – you want to emerge from the darkness
And you give me all the credit.

No – it is your own courage
                your own realization
                your power
                your energy that is being sparked.

It is your life that you will claim and nurture
The life within you –
With your own talents –
This light – it is your own
Keep your flame lit – until your last breath*!*

This fire is your source of energy
                    creativity
                  spirit
                    reflection

This is the fire that stars are made of! Transform yourself –
Set your sights high, wide and far beyond yesterday's dream.
This light knows no limit.
It shines beyond the horizon

Go forward
You have a destination waiting for its discovery
Places unseen
Give yourself new vision

Re-create yourself
Face the wilderness, carve out a new existence,
As the brave warriors and forefathers boldly took fate into their own hands
It was within them – it is within you.
You are a part of them – strong, independent, survivor

Do you know who you are, who you descended from?
Do you understand?

A Point of Light

Do not focus on the points of light – use the light.
Do not blind yourself staring at me –
See what has been bestowed upon yourself
And what lies ahead

Use the point of light – turn back, find another road
Rise up in body and spirit

I'm blessed to be light – and bright – the perfection,
brilliance and excellence have dazzled and thrilled all
that watch – I'm no magician –

I'm all action – I shine – I travel faster than you can
comprehend – I am light.

Act, brave soul, now, there is so much to learn.
Life is all around – go, live, with all talents, all senses,
go in every direction, find yourself where you can soar
to new heights.

You have lived among shadows
Your talents dormant
There is beauty in all you think and do
Look at me – I'm just an example of talent that flows in
abundance
Begin, I command you, begin to fulfill your destination!

There is no easy way to face me
I'm in front of you, facing you, just you, just me,
Nothing can hide from me, a genius of purity,
I see, clearly

Something is wrong and it needs fixing
Your existence depends on it

There is only one truth that stands upright
Live in truths – the battle will always favor you –

Glow, then a spark, then the flame
Set this world ablaze with your courage to live

It is all there, all within you"

Snowy Day in Houston

Focus on the natural flow from within.
Be at one with nature, so you can
Seek life's true secrets.

This morning, and as day moves forward, I have watched from up high, almost thirty storeys above the ground, and reflected as this uncommon event opens my thoughts and influences my mood. I have turned the chair and footrest around, so I can face outward from the rounded corner window where family photos are framed and organized – a display of history, close bonds, affection, and life. I sit with legs extended, covered by father's shawl, taking part in this unusual scene – within the safe and secure environment of home – wanting to converse with nature today.

All day, the flakes are a special visitor – I know not when I will see him again, yet I'm hypnotized by the blaze, something came from where, all of a sudden? The event calmed me, silenced me.

Such a performance the snow gave me on nature's stage – a natural green background of trees, wintry white skies. Breeze was defined through the millions of flakes, floating, lingering then rushing, flowing like fluid, swirling, rising, greeting me at the window, then dancing and twisting, blustering and swarming, layers of movement in opposite direction, bringing open space alive.

I didn't want it to end. I had to watch it all – the flakes were telling me, "This is our time" and "Something special is in the air for you."

The white sky did not rush or race to the ground – it wound its way down as though enjoying the flight. It captured me, then it was gone. Quicker than it came, it vanished, leaving me wanting more.

Snow, please return, finish telling me your message! It was too brief a visit. Something so natural, so uplifting and purifying to my spirit.

Watching you today, snow, almost like a stranger to me, seeing you through the eyes of a renewed soul, for moments took me somewhere else away from time and agenda.

Part of my "emotional journey" – an ocean so deep, warm and cold currents, the never-disappointing sky offering rare glimpses every time I look up.

I did not know when you were going to arrive. Snow, how did you keep me so enthralled? All I did was look at you, I felt it and I knew. It was a freezing day, full of road hazards, chills in the air – how was I warmed by the sight of you all around me, I could see nothing else? A magical event.

I am still, in one place, yet I travel all over the universe of my own being – I visit energy, determination, spirit, strength, perseverance, all paths that allow me to renew, restore, to find myself. This state of mind, today, I thank the snow for it, to find the words.

Everything around me has opened up to me – as though I'm discovering life, spending time choosing to live, for the first time. Has it taken me this long to begin? Why?

As I write these words, the sun is out and is setting. I am still sitting at the window. Today while the snow was starting in early morning here, I said two things specifically to myself – grab my yellow pad and stand at the window.

Also, read Robert Frost's poem[1] from the book Daddy gave me – back in 1997. You'd signed it and quoted Iqbal.[2] Then I started to take notes. About the flakes themselves, about you. Today I had planned to write a letter for your birthday.

Several years ago while we were out to dinner, you reached out to me through loving words of a father – you painted a picture for me with these words and explained to me how my life could be – that my world would open up. I have put all my faith in your words, spoken and

---

[1] The Road Not Taken, a poem by Robert Frost (1874-1963), San Francisco, CA USA
[2] 'Stronger the Wind – Higher the Eagle Flies' written by my father, referring to Allama Muhammad Iqbal (1877-1938), India, who often wrote about the eagle's character symbolically

through your eyes, from that day. I have been so blessed to have you as my father, as part of you.

What matters to me now – has evolved through this emotional journey. Intentionally, I wanted to reflect on Frost's poem today. At this point in time, how I respond to that poem, it's almost a "yardstick" – where am I now? Who am I? – metaphorically.

What I got from Robert Frost today – that has made all the difference – is to try the path, and going on. To try and make a change.

Having the mind and heart connection between father and daughter, the care and concern, has been my truest and deepest blessing in this lifetime. Our work together – it's integrated through our bond and my faith in you – it has shaped me and given meaning to my current and future existence. I have so much more to learn, so far to go, hurdles to jump over…pure work, nothing less. We will succeed together.

If I could have anything from life, I would choose to feel alive, to know good luck like a good friend; I would choose to stay positive and strong, to think independently, to have blessed health and discipline, to achieve success through our mutual goals, to live a life by giving love, to be respected, to have a full heart and to experience travel in rare dimensions.

All of the business meetings – whenever I have been with you – you stand out as the brightest, most confident, alert, original, clearest, best, the strongest mind – I cannot help but feel pride for you as my father – it magnifies at these times.

I ask myself, how can I ever be that good, why am I not as good, why couldn't I see it all from the beginning – what blocked my view? You always say to forget it and move forward, no regrets. My mental errors do linger like an old scar even though life is offering me a better chance with goodness and blessing on my side. For now, I put faith in seeing clearer and faith in going to where I belong.

I would be nothing without you; none of my current life could be possible. You are the blessing that reveals itself most at this stage in my life; more than anything else.

I was a fool to take so much in life for granted, blindly, not understanding the true worth of anything. It came to

me through time and continues to enter into my awareness. I still have a long way to climb, as I study myself and strive for renewal. Please forgive me.
All of your love and time spent, I treasure deep within, a place that has a need but never openly asks, a place somehow not able to reach easily.

It was snow that today brought out these feelings towards father. Now that the snow is gone, the sky is dark and day draws to an end, I am left reading one final page of notes from the yellow pad, all written around mid-day during the time when this mood was in creation.

What did the snow tell me today? It said, enjoy a rare moment. Start writing. Focus on the natural flow from within.

Be at one with nature, so you can seek life's true secrets.

Contentment and internal peace is within grasp.

The snow said, I won't disappoint you, here is a gift for you today. Life will transform you when you use all senses, and you will give of self in as many ways.

This is how you will discover your rhythm.

The snow told me, I am visual delight, expressive, dynamic, surprising, vivid. You are warm, safe inside, you are free, and good things are coming.

The patterns, at times heavy, at times light, slow, fast, gusting through horizontally, dense with larger flakes – just like life.

I used a markedly different day that lingered enough, just enough, to express this letter.

Your daughter, Sofia
December 2009

A Test of Faith

*My richness runs through these veins, nowhere else.
Can I become a jewel?*

On my way to Alabama – it was Father's Day – I reflected while sitting on the plane, flying somewhere up high, closer to the blue that I turn to, each evening during my favorite time of day – the twilight – the time when the sun has gone down, and from my balcony I watch colors change, light fades, the first star appears, rays flash across the sky in the slowest motion. I wonder, does everyone capture this beauty as I do, a new canvas each and every day, to reflect with silent joy?

I regret missing Father's Day at parents' home over the weekend, yet welcome the chance to go and make a living. Graciously over these months, you have given to me, a way to keep my dignity and to focus on our effort – I would like you to know that the tumultuous pressures within me were eased with your steadfast generosity and understanding.

My mood has been altered so much recently – a journey into the future seems to fulfill every emotion. There was a day not that long ago, looking back, I realize now that my inner strength knew no peace.

I was in the desert, was I lost there? Which way was I to go? A few passersby, a few clues, all pointed in different directions. Then I realized, do they even know where they point me to? Will I ever find the way?

I tasted one glass of water only – yet every drop has evaporated – it was only a mirage. Will I ever dive into my own pool? This soul thirsts helplessly for another gulp, a pitcher full – I needed help – I needed someone to travel with me, lead the way in this desolate, isolated, dry desert with only sky, moon, colors, hollow sound. My sense of direction faded, I'm diving into darkness, I ask, where can you possibly be?

Will I unfold? Do I just wander aimlessly in this wild and hostile terrain, for days and nights? Does the heart just collapse from this weary isolation?

I ask, where is my faith? Is it here, is this the test of faith? What's the answer? What's the best way? I need a little luck.

Does luck enter the desert? Or is it lucky to have me here, captured, victorious?

Oasis

Barely conscious. Crackling heat, blistered feet. Withered spirit, knocked down but not out. I'm lost, I've wandered, I've crawled on this scalding ground, I've just laid there in the dust, looking for the beauty in this glorious sky – any time of day it sends me nourishment that has sustained me.

I reach to my forefathers – please help me – strengthen me – guide me. What am I made of? They told me of courage, stamina, aura, nobility, depth, dignity, loyalty, boldness, pride, never giving up, second to none, faith. All of the qualities that overcomes all odds, that draw others near. Why oh why, then, am I alone, lost in this wilderness, this barrenness? How did I get here?

There is an oasis somewhere; a place I will find myself, faith will lead me there.

The oasis awaits. Oasis, how long have you waited?

Did you start thinking I've perished, that I wouldn't show up? You felt my calling, my tears – help me, find me, I need you, the way is toiling on me, I feel weakened, my desire faded, I admit this only to you, oasis – lift me up from this dreariness that has tricked me into liking the desert – the softness of pure sand, the heat glazing me as I cry – there's nothing left.

I wait for what? What do I value? There's nothing, no one that is mine. Yet the heart remains full, pounding strongly, steady beat – this heart flows with giving, loving, brightness, restored, full.

Faith exists. I exist for faith. I won't give up. My richness runs through these veins, nowhere else.
No witnesses, no listeners. It's all within. The bond that has been created, not always obvious, but beyond obvious. This journey enriches me, challenges my core,

my consciousness. Self realization approaches gradually.

Oasis cannot be seen – it is felt, it is valued, something taken for granted when in our very possession. Without it, we're lost.

Constantly tested, I look to my own name. Sofia. Am I living up to my own name? This name, synonymous with knowledge, insight, judgment, wise course of action, even godly wisdom.

Am I able to realize my own potential? Am I beginning to understand life? Nature? Matter? Reason? Truth? Am I of action? Or words? Can I become a jewel? Or water that just vaporizes? I choose the strength of a diamond.

Together, seeking a common destination, our effort makes me feel lucky about having such a father. Getting to know you, my father, I have gotten to know about myself. What I'm in need of, I've discovered, is there. Within. I have to search hard and long and deep within. It's unique yet it's there.

Now – having returned from Alabama and seeing business activity and meeting new clients – I continue to give, and desire to help another who has suffered, in hopes of making an impact, even to just one. In so many ways, realization of my own blessings manifest during these moments, and inspire me to share of self.

I asked myself during these recent travels, who am I, what do I want, what makes me so lucky in this life, and if I had a wish, what would it be? I wrote my answers while on the plane.

Who am I? I am…one of <u>them</u>. Tribe.

What do I want? I would like to show you, or for you to see in me, that there was something good in me, perhaps some reflection of you, or others from past generations, that I also possess, that I have discovered within me.

What makes me so lucky in this life? That I've had a father for more than 46 years of my life, and he is truly the individual who has deep understanding, who has shaped my life more now…a guide, an inspiration, a rare excellence. Now I see.

If I had a wish, it would be that I could have worked with you my entire career, not just this past decade.

I said I'd come this morning yet I had to write this letter – yesterday I was planning to do so, but time was taken by work.

Your daughter, Sofia

Moments Worth Waiting For

...there is a way...
...and you will be there to glow in that light...

Pains

Worries, Concerns

When do you end?

Why does this mind constantly remind of the world and its troubles?

Where do we go to release it all, to regain energy and comfort, to find beauty, to enjoy several moments of peace?

This day, drifting through, activities that have personal feelings attached –
I find myself mostly quiet, silent during the day.

The evening sky, summer sky, warmed pool water,
Soothes me – unwinding and relaxed, lap after lap –
Still able to maintain my discipline, moving freely
Yet with deliberation – the years have been generous to my active and restless spirit.

The same hawk – city hawk – the same one who as I stood frozen – dove directly toward me then applied brakes in mid-air – after getting close enough to see my human silhouette – I enjoy these wings where no others go – how did you get here – you are at home here yet I imagine deserts, mountains, high rocks, peaks you've flown to.

I swim on, lap after lap, maybe an hour, maybe longer – slowly, feeling the pace, my own pace, thinking that new plans are possible – there is a way if I can envision them.

Oh sky, the blue, the veil of thin cloud I love so much, I am glad I waited to see your colors change as the sun closes out its daylight.

I'm floating on my back, looking up at you, I see only you – this is the moment I had been waiting for – you dazzle me again – my eyes moisten thanks to you – so lovely to look at – the gift you deliver – takes away my pain, my sorrow, my tension, all my troubles and defeats left behind even for an instant or longer – the brilliant scheme of colors – each time a new portrait of evening, always new, always renewing me.

Sky, I know what you are telling me – "the moment you've been working towards – will be worth the wait, and you will be there to glow in that light, you will celebrate that moment, it will receive your adoration, it will sense your appreciation." It will be.

Dearest Path

The more you give, the further you will go on this path.
The dust on my feet from this path -
May I always remain dusty.

Pen in hand, I write.

Given a vision, I strive towards my goal.

With knowledge, I grow.

With love, I survive.

This path, I travel.

Excerpts from a Dialog

The path expresses to me, "Welcome, again."

I reply, "So you understand that I'm in the mood to talk with you?"

"Yes," the path responds. "It will be the first time we've really spoken. What is it that brings on this desire to communicate with me?"

I explain, "I wanted to examine where I've been, just to reflect. Perhaps you in turn, will tell me what you see. Do you remember when I started on this path?"

"Yes," a warm reply. "You and your shiny new bike, it was 2008, maybe March – you'd bring your basket with bread, camera, phone, drinks…all sorts of accessories."

"Now, you come alone, no basket, no baggage, you come…then you leave. Perhaps, you've lost the enjoyment of coming here."

"No," I say, "You misjudge me. I've shed them away so I can partner with you directly. All I need is to focus on you."

"For a while, you were not coming. I miss you."

"Yes, the storm prevented me."

"Storm? I cannot recall…storms never made you stay away before."

"It was inside me – I couldn't contain it any longer. Was I saying, CHANGE, WORLD!! Was I unfulfilled and tired of waiting? Was I praying for "I need you now"? Perhaps even more, unwritten, unspoken, heartfelt matters of the soul."

So here I am again, renewed, healed, as though I've arrived on my wild black stallion, long mane unkempt, in full blaze,
Holding on with arms hugging around his neck, in perfect union
No more fear, no saddle, no reins, no stirrups
Just me and stallion…take me there, I tell him
Without a word
In a language only known between us.

I say to you, "This is the path I choose."

The path wonders, "Why me? I'm dusty, I'm worn, cracked on the surface,
I'm no beautiful stream, there are no canals and no hilly views here, no vast views.
I'm not popular – I lay empty most of the time.
I'm weathered, covered in gravel or sand,
I don't wander through the countryside
I just go in a circle, over and over again.
Where's the attraction?"

The path continues, "I'm nothing to look at…yet you keep your eyes on me. Every now and then, I notice that you look up – straight up."

"You come here, you go in circles, same direction, there's no one here but you, it's the same thing
Why do you keep coming back to this lonesome trail?"

"You wear such a masterful disguise," I say after a long pause.

"The trees line and adorn you wherever you go – you lead the way.
You take me forward.
Nothing is ever the same.
Like days of the week, I go round and round,
I learn your texture, the width, the turns, the weather, the seasons.

With you, I go, I move, I act
Sometimes, I'm exposed, you shelter me with greenery.
I keep going, I learn to love the circles

They are never the same – a new breeze, a strong gust, a sprinkle of rain, the golden shimmering through the leaves…
You give me so many gifts.

"Your disguise is what calls to me –
You are alone so I travel with you.

When I first started, I was unsure if I could even turn one corner.
I had no idea how far I had come until I reflected, just now.
With you.
I am so attached to you.

I know your turns, the cracks, the holes, the bumps, the slopes, your curves.
As time goes on, I keep my eyes on you more, anticipating obstacles, detours, near-collisions.

I stay alert. I find balance. My mind clears.
I find answers.

My heart races, my lungs fill, I exert, I coast, I glide,
And every now and then, yes, I take my eyes off of this path and look straight upwards."

The path assures me,
"You have a friend in me.
I promise you, I can give you what you seek in me.
The more you give, the further you will go on this path."

"Give me your energy, leave your tracks all over me, your imprint – I'll strengthen you, your stamina will increase, your heart will beat in rhythm with what you're willing to put on the path.

You have wheels – now ride."

The path asks, "Can you reflect on your experiences here?"

I elaborate –

> "There was a day. It was one of those days that I pushed myself hard. Early afternoon. My goal was ten circles. A hot, summer day."

The path responds,

    "You can ride when the day cools off – why then?"

I reflect, "How will I feel the toiling of so many others, who give their backs and their brows, and work in the relentless conditions…how will I know them unless I also dedicate my efforts in this condition? I have to share something of theirs. They are brave, resilient, tough – they have built everything so we can be fed, be clothed, be sheltered. It is their thankless and tireless lives we ignore. I ride for them, in the middle of the summer day. They deserve respect and dignity."

"The heat is a strain; it cleanses and purifies all emotions. It develops feelings beyond the parched throat, burning skin, swimming head. I wanted to stop – I had little left in me, I thought. The shadows were growing darker, I felt drained, I was bent over from fatigue…I said – no more."

I continued…"Among all this greenery, the darkening shadows cast within the coverage of thick foliage and woods, as I came through, hot breeze cooling me, I had to stop pedaling and just give my senses a short break, as though to unwind for the day. I looked forward, into the distance, loosening the intensity of my focus on this path…I'm done. That's it."

I continue my narration,
"From right to left, within sight but out of arm's reach
Was the bluest butterfly, to cool me.

Then, the blue jay left to right, smoothing flight to another branch
The clarity of such color lifted me up
So I faced straight upwards, and again…blue.

Among all the green and shadows…the delight of living blue given to me.

Precious gifts have saved me when needed the most. Stored in me. Thank you. Thank you. Thank you. Tearfully. Thank you."

The dust on my feet from this path –
May I always remain dusty.

Dearest path, you are my gem. You are tucked away
secretly in this big world,

You offer refuge, you make my heart beat strong,
You challenge me, through you I understand.
I still have a long way to go.

I look into your eyes,
you look into mine,
today, now…
I am seeking.
And this once, I will find myself.

To my father.
With love, Sofia

Re-emergence

Soar higher as the wind blows harder against you
See all horizons

Dry eyes, blurry vision, awaken from the night's rest.
Wintry, cloudy sullen days, gray everywhere
Same moment of opening my eyes, facing the sky through my window
The hawk flew by, from the left – straight across, swift gliding

Suddenly my body obeyed – get up. Rise*!*

I was startled by my own reaction, this command that
reached me the very second I awoke

So naturally

I heard the hawk saying to me
"Watch me today – see me now in flight
As I soar higher and higher – this cold winter wind
facing me, challenging me in all directions

I am solitary, the sky – where I belong, up here
High, towards this expanse, free
Navigating upwards, seeing all around
My wings, my character, this oneness with sky
These keen senses, majestic wingspan, open
The entire expanse, entire horizon, belongs to me.

No limits.

Oh life, dare me, I will show you what I'm created for –
my spirit is my guide. Deserts, mountains, faraway, the
highest peaks – all within my domain.

Awaken today, rise now, the time has come

I'm here to show you
There's a chill – come outside, feel its effect
This moment, join me
Just take off, let this winter wind carry you up
Face the odds, the currents whirling – use them

See yourself up here, this view, this sky
Far from the ground, so unlike that hard surface, that grind
Soar higher as the wind blows harder against you
See all horizons, 360 degrees

This is no ordinary day!
The darkness was cast, the chill, the damp
Watch the brightness, the silhouette,
The disk, emerge from beneath the gray sky
Soon, too bright to look at
What a welcome, the warmth, the day all of a sudden new
Restored.
Each moment, in its own way, a gift to sustain you,
Nourish you, save you
You did not perish
It did not take forever
Now, you see, you listen, at one with life itself."

I stop at the table by the curved window.
Same photos of family – four generations.
All eyes meeting mine, never before did I get such response.

Grandmother – looking into her eyes – she's saying
You are my granddaughter – part of this noble vein of gold,

Mother says, my faith is your faith, one and same, enduring,

Grandfather – says –
When you need strength, call to me, I am courage
Fearless
Chivalry exists.
What I possess, lives in your father, lives in you.
All yours.
Oh brother, how long have you had to wait? I sense your smile.
A new warmth, all over again. Children – bright, lively.

They all say, we're with you, find your way,
The sun has emerged from the clouds,
And you, too have re-emerged
And you too, shall soar –

Your courage to change direction, to face the headwind,
Make the necessary steps back –
To find yourself again – your existence depended on it –
You are renewed, you are glowing, you are warm, soft
You are more alive

It is the reality.

Still standing at that table
Finally, I say

Oh wise man, so brief your answers
I poured my heart to you
Your responses so short, so many times
So stark
So truthful, over and over to me
All you said was

> You chose it
> Go back; you're on the wrong road
> Walk faster
> Keep going, don't stop
> Forget the past
> Focus on yourself
> Time is precious
> No regrets
> Use your brain
> Open the mind
> Fly higher
> Moderation
> Until your last breath
> Solve it
> Paint

Write
Discover it
Find it
Use me
Life will open up to you
I will never let you down, as long as I'm here
You'll know
One truth.

These words, few at a time, on and on
Patiently over my lifetime
Answers to all my anxieties,
Wisdom, Love, the guide…

Answers to the complexity of all things
Telling me – fly with me, come with me

Welcome home, he says, silently

It's me, I reply.

I'm listening.

We walk side by side; I lean my head on his right shoulder.

Credits and Acknowledgments

Additional thanks to every true friend I have had and to the children in my life. I acknowledge you.

And to the unappreciated, most beautiful, minds.

About the Author

Sofia Khan grew up in the world of international oil exploration, with its cyclical nature of boom times and downturns. Her father traveled extensively and dedicated his entire career to the advancement of technology for oil discovery. His work and enduring commitment in the quest to find oil influenced the environment she lived in.

Ms. Khan's family moved from one hemisphere to the other, lived in and traveled to both developed and underdeveloped countries. She has received an education far beyond the schools and degrees on record. In spite of earning an M.B.A. from the University of Houston and a B.A. Managerial Studies degree from Rice University, and with over twenty five years of securities and insurance experience, Sofia Khan is most interested in the energy challenge to help solve what could become a severe global energy crisis.

Sofia Khan has supported her father since 2001 on the creation of direct oil detection technology as the means to the energy solution - she is Vice President of Nonlinear Seismic Imaging, Inc., a company that has patents on this revolutionary technology.

Global leaders recognize that each nation is interconnected, in which no one is an "island" that should be left behind. Irrespective of how much effort is put in, the world cannot get away from fossil fuels easily. With an increased and stable supply of resources, developing nations will shift towards higher industrialization, improved standards of living and increased food production – a win-win for all parties.

As the world's population increases and nations desire a better standard of living, the world will continue to face uncertainty unless the imbalance between resource distribution and population is solved. The oil industry needs a new and highly diagnostic technology that directly detects and maps the hydrocarbon reservoir fluids and reservoir properties, rather than the subsurface structure.

Nonlinear Seismic Imaging technology differentiates Sofia Khan from everyone. It solves practical challenges, is cost-effective in that it requires very little additional capital, improves recovery from the existing fields, identifies and locates oil reservoirs that have not been mapped, is fairly simple for its market application, and will provide results and images that illuminate only the oil in the subsurface and not structural features.

Sofia Khan wrote this book for everyone, everywhere, about believing in the human spirit, courage, and hope.